The Wisdom of Grief

2021

GOLDEN DRAGONFLY PRESS

FIRST PRINT EDITION, July 2021
FIRST EBOOK EDITION, July 2021

Copyright © 2021 by Amanda Brutus-Phillips

All rights reserved.
No part of this publication may be reproduced
or transmitted in any form or by any means, electronic
or otherwise, without prior written permission
by the copyright owner.

ISBN: 978-1-7330099-5-9

Library of Congress Control Number: 2021935119

Printed on acid-free paper.
First published in the United States of America
by Golden Dragonfly Press, 2021.

www.goldendragonflypress.com

To all those souls experiencing loss and grief.
This is for you.

I dedicate this book to my children Jay and Janaya.
I love you.

Contents

My Date With Grief 1

How I Feel in My Grief 9

Daily Musings 11

Transformation During Grief 45

Acknowledgments 61

My Date With Grief

"Death will come, always out of season. It is the command of the Great Spirit, and all nations and people must obey."

—Big Elk

"I love you." Those were the last words I said to him through text. Everything seemed so normal, normal conversation, normal night, normal him, normal me. Yet there was nothing normal about it at all, we just couldn't see the next 20 minutes into the future when normal became a nightmare. I came to recognize this when the autumn of my life came suddenly and tragically in the summer of what was supposed to be my season of joy. After returning from my trip to Thailand, I excitedly prepared for the return of my husband and daughters from their trip in the Caribbean visiting family. They were waiting to board their flight home and I couldn't wait to see them. Three weeks had felt like a lifetime. It was 11:08 pm and I recall being in my bedroom doing the most normal of things, folding clothes and putting away things from the suitcase I had just unpacked from my Thailand trip. In the midst of folding and unpacking, my daughter called me to check in; they were at the airport waiting to board the plane. In that conversation she related to me that dad was having pain in his leg, it was the first time I had heard that he was having any issues. We continued our conversation and I promised her that I would talk to dad and find out what was going on. Minutes later, I began a stream of text with my husband, I asked him how he was doing and he replied that he was feeling lethargic and that his thigh muscle was sore. He convinced me that he was fine and that he would be okay once he got on the plane.

Our conversation drifted to our excitement to see each other again, he replied how he was looking forward to feeling my warmth and how much he needed a hug. I thought that was the sweetest thing I've heard all day. We continued our stream of text and ended with I love you babes, see you in a few hours. It was 11:25 pm and

I went back to folding my clothes and unpacking my suitcase as I listened to music. Twenty minutes later I received a frantic phone call from my hysterical daughter on the other side, "Mom something is wrong with dad, he had a seizure as he tried to get up." Those words rocked my world, along with the words from the doctor about 45 minutes later saying, "I'm sorry your husband has died." At that moment I was confused as to what was going on and yet through that confusion a tormented shriek tore through my whole being. It was the worst pain, feeling, moment I have ever experienced in my life. At that moment I felt this surrealness, like I wasn't part of this world anymore, I was in between planes, in a void of some space I could not name. There was no ground for me to touch with my feet, no walls to give me boundaries, only space and that space was more than I could bear, it felt too empty. There was no one to hold me, to catch my tears, no one to tell me that I was dreaming. I felt so alone.

I thought we had time. In an instant, my life changed. I'd been rocked, blindsided, and the earth had opened up and swallowed whatever plans I had, whatever plans we had. What I felt now was uncertainty, fear, torment, and shock. I simply could not believe that the man I loved who I was speaking with at 11:25 pm was now gone at 1:00 am. Surely this was a cruel joke but it was not, it was all too real and the most bewildering part about it all was my trip to Thailand. In October of 2016, I had registered for a course in Thailand titled The Art of Dying for July 2017. It was a course that taught the practices of the Buddhist Book of the Dead. I remember talking to him one night about the course, relaying how amazing the course was and that when he died I would help him cross over to the other side. He responded by saying "are you saying I'm going to die?" I joked it off and said, "of course not, I just want you to know that when your time does come I will help you cross over." I had no idea that two weeks later I would be doing exactly that. I was in such disbelief. I simply could not believe that upon returning from a course on death and dying that I would need to utilize what I had learned for my own husband. How could this be?

Hours later I found myself on a plane to Trinidad, I cried every step of the way. I didn't care that people looked at me strangely; I was in pain, mourning, in shock, and the tears had no end. I just wanted to be with my girls, to hold them, and try to reassure them it was going to be okay. But that was I lie I kept conjuring up, it wasn't okay and how could I reassure two teenagers of anything when they just witness the passing of their father. In the end, all I could do once I saw them was hold them and cry. I had nothing more to give than my own tears. I felt for them, could feel their tired exhausted bodies still confused from the last 24 hours. Confused seemed to be what we all felt and sick to our bellies. I gathered enough of myself up to do what people do in these situations, identify the body, make funeral arrangements, get all necessary documents, and pretend like life didn't just sucker punch me in the gut. It was the hardest thing I had to do when every part felt like I was a zombie walking around in a post-apocalyptic world. Nothing made sense. The cause of death, a massive blood clot to the lungs.

The girls and I made the tough decision to bury him in his country that he loved so much so the plans were made to bury him in Tobago. We all knew it was what he would want, his soul knew, he never got on that plane to come home. He was home. It seemed like the days went by in a blur, I could not breathe, eat, nor sleep, and the beginnings of PTSD had begun to take over my body. Fear gripped me and I felt myself suffocating like I was dying, death had shown its face and no one was immune, I no longer felt safe. All I wanted to do was go home, as if home held something that could save me, but it was something I knew and I needed to feel something familiar. I left Tobago feeling as if I'd been betrayed by life, I couldn't trust it anymore. How could I? Not after it had ripped the dreams of two souls who had just recommitted their lives to each other again. We thought we had time, but we didn't have time. Soon the stewing of anger began to bubble within me, I was damn angry. My anger was not limited. I felt anger towards my husband for leaving me, angry with God for taking him, angry with myself and angry with life. Why did God always take the good ones? Why? I needed to understand, I needed this to make sense. A rawness that I've never felt before began to bloom.

Weeks went by and still I lived in that "it can't be place." My heart was finding it very hard to believe that the person I had spent the last 24 years with was no longer with me, living and breathing. Everywhere I turned in the house there was a reminder of him, an article of clothing, a picture, his shoes, his phone, car, in some strange way seeing those things gave me a false sense that he was still here, that my normal was still well, normal. But it was the sunken look in my eyes whenever I had the courage to look at myself in the mirror, my tearstained cheeks, the pain and hurt in my daughter's eyes, and the constant anxiety attacks that now assaulted my body day and night that reminded me that nothing was normal anymore. I had entered into a war zone and it was my life.

Each day I asked myself, "how do I move on, how do I live this new life?" I did not want to do this life anymore, the sheer pain was unbearable. The one thing that pulled me back from the ledge was my daughters. The suffering and trauma they had witnessed were enough, I needed to protect them from further pain. The trauma of seeing their father die right in front of them will never leave their innocent minds, it will be replayed like a broken record for a long time to come. The insecurity they are feeling as if they are waiting for the other shoe to drop also scared me as I felt myself waiting for the same thing. Maybe I was next. I know how morbid it sounds but every day was a struggle to not feel like I too was dying, that the grim reaper in some way had it in for me too. There was no trust for life anywhere, I felt separated from life and God. I felt empty. The concern I saw in their eyes for me and the question they ask me continually with fear in the background was always "Mom are you okay?" I could tell that they were afraid that something might happen to me too and in all honesty, the level of fear I was carrying around in my mind drove me to that same conclusion. I knew it was the panic attacks talking and the PTSD. Yet it felt so real but I knew I had to fake it and say, "yes baby, mom is okay." They had been through so much, what more could their fragile hearts take I could no lay another layer at their doorstep? My own limits had been reached for I knew I had arrived at what seemed the edge of my existence. The loss of a mother two years ago now followed by the sudden death of a husband. What was the universe doing? What message was it sending me? And the question that just wouldn't leave my heart was "Why?" I knew it was the wrong question but it was the only one my grieving heart wanted to know.

In the midst of it all, any trust I'd ever had of the present moment or of God slipped away, the same way life could so easily slip away from our grip. I had more questions than answers but still, I continued to ask them hoping maybe someday an answer will come. I teetered back and forth to loving God and being angry at God. Our relationship during the first year took me to a place I never imagined seeing myself in, a faith crisis. In the first year of my grief, I walked along a dark path filled with disbelief and denial which held me captive with uncertainty and fear. I felt reduced to being a baby unable to figure anything out. The only thing I had the courage to do was to exist, no expectations, no planning, no pressure, just to be here and now feeling all the pain and grief that were now part of my everyday life. It happened to be the most devastating and painful thing I've ever experience.

One of the only things that I had inspiration for was writing. It is through journaling during moments of sadness, fear, anger, pain, and in some rare moments, happiness that I share here with you. There were also some moments of laughter that came in between the deep sorrows that helped me shed some light on the darkest time of my life. These short snippets allowed me gracefully to attend to all the feelings that were rummaging through me, to hold each one tenderly and with care and to let the light pass over me soothing the darkness away. I am ever grateful to a God that I love passionately even when I am angry and cannot understand the "why's" of life.

Most wandering through the streets of grief want to rush back to a busy life they knew, rush back to feeling normal, and rush out of feeling the heaviness that grief brings with it. My hope as you read this book is that you will find some inspiration as you go through your season of grief with me as your companion. Your experience will surely be different from mine and that is to be expected, I honor all of your experiences as I do mine.

This book is a collection of my deepest feelings, thoughts, and affirmations that arose in this first year of grief. It is raw, honest, and authentic. I find that this experience of death, dying, and grief cannot be sugar-coated, and I came to learn how to accept the range of emotions that I felt. I learned along the way that opening myself fully to the experience brought many gifts into my life, gifts I am still unwrapping.

It's about learning forgiveness, welcoming love, kindness, and compassion into your life during this time. It's about being open, receptive and trusting in the process of grief. It's about befriending the fear you feel and the darkness that covers you. It's about welcoming transformation and the expansion that can occur during this time. But most importantly it's about leaning into the moment and being gentle. We often forget how powerful it can be to embrace stillness and do less so we can feel and remind ourselves of our humanness.

This book is about honoring our beloved who has passed on with a private heartfelt ceremony of our feelings, it's about saying goodbye to the fat elephants in the room; guilt, fear, anger, loneliness, depression, and all the other emotions that come along with feeling grief after the death of a loved one.

This book is about having the courage to see death as a beginning rather than an ending if you can allow it. What this book isn't, is a way for you to throw your grief to the side and ignore it. It isn't a book to replace your own wisdom and intuitive sense of what's right and wrong for you. It isn't a book dictating what you should or shouldn't do, let's not bring "should" into our conversation here.

I want you to connect to your heart space and feel into its very own wisdom so you can courageously experience your own state of being authentic.

If you have gone through grief of any kind, I hope these sayings will help guide you in your own unique way to a healing place that is right for you and perhaps give you inspiration to write your own heartfelt views, thoughts, and feelings.

Thank you for joining me on my personal journey of grief. We are all walking each other through life's many terrains. May love guide, hold, and keep the eternal light ever lit in the chamber of your heart despite loss. Many blessings to you.

How I Feel in My Grief

THE VERY BEGINNING

What's the use	Anxious	Feeling lost
Unable to trust life	Overwhelmed	Breathless
No joy	Sadness	Afraid
Angry	Hurt	Pain
Close heart	Tears	Broken
Depressed	Heavy	Uncertain
Panic	Separated	Alone
Faithless	Denial	Tired

Daily Musings

"The Lord is close to the brokenhearted and saves those who are crushed in spirit."
—Psalms 38:18

I cannot remember which came first, the denial or the shock. Somehow, they both seem to merge into one big horrible moment.

It's unimaginable, this feeling of grief. It's like the deepest, heaviest weight pressing on your heart squeezing out all the old you've been hiding and all the new heartaches developing.

I cried for months, unable to stop the torrential downflow from stopping. In truth, I could not stop them. Each tear was a diamond honoring the love that existed between us and secretly the fear I felt inside.

It's strange to hold joy and grief within the same plane. One moment is filled with so much sadness of loss and the other moment an eruption of laughter at a simple joke being told. Life is still present.

I didn't understand why the world didn't stop to mourn with me. Why people still continued to live, laugh and have a good time. It was strange to be around life when death had paid me a visit.

Grief is like an archeologist who comes with her shovel and all the other excavation tools ready to dig up old fossils long buried.

SCREAM
Let the
BrOkEnNeSs
OUT

"You will lose someone you can't live without, and your heart will be badly broken, and the bad news is that you never completely get over the loss of your beloved. But this is also the good news. They live forever in your broken heart that doesn't seal back up. And you come through. It's like having a broken leg that never heals perfectly — that still hurts when the weather gets cold, but you learn to dance with the limp."

—Anne Lamott

Can I trust anything that I feel during grief? What is real and authentic and what is a fabrication of my mind wanting to deflect the pain.

There is a space somewhere in this grief where it's just empty space surrounding me. Void of any emotions. It's just stillness and silence. A listening. My soul is listening.

My mind wants to understand why. Why did he have to die? I tell myself why is not the right question, there are no answers that can justify this agony. I have only God.

People say you're so strong. I want them to look deep inside my heart and then say that.

It is hard to see it coming, the unexpected moment that completely blindsides you to a breathless whisper of sheer pain.

I distrusted life after you died and felt separated from God. Oh, what a horrible time that was.

The shock of your death led me down a road of insecurities. I trusted nothing and no one. Not even life.

EXPOSE THE ANGER YOU FEEL INSIDE. EACH RELEASE BRINGS HEALING

"There is a sacredness in tears. They are not the mark of weakness, but of power. They speak more eloquently than ten thousand tongues. They are the messengers of overwhelming grief, of deep contrition, and of unspeakable love."

—Washington Irving

I thought I would be prepared, okay with death when it came to those I love the most. Instead, fear ran up my legs and curled its tail into a sleeping position. I wasn't prepared.

Death comes to level out the playing field amongst all the divisions in the world. It doesn't discriminate, it takes all, the rich, the poor, the white, and the black. Death is the great equalizer.

I was filled with raw anger; it rose like yellow bile in my bloodstream blinding me in this grief. I was angry at him for dying, angry at God for taking him, and angry with myself for being angry at all. I just let it be and give myself to it. Eventually, it too dissolved and I realize the anger is a necessary part of the grief process.

I am uncertain of what is next, my breath, my footsteps, my life. How do I pick up what is left of my life? They are all now in tattered pieces.

No one tells you how painful and raw the heart actually feels when your beloved dies. One must go through it to know and understand.

Silence lived amongst the internal chaos taking place in my life. How could there be silence in the midst of chaos? Yet the silence continued and the chaos deepens. No God answering back, only the silence in between the tears, the ravaging heartbeat, the tormented mind. Only thick silence like the dead had taken up residence in the long corridor of the living.

CRY A THOUSAND TEARS FOR THE GRIEF YOU ARE FEELING EACH DROP BELONGS TO GOD

"While grief is fresh, every attempt to divert only irritates. You must wait till it's digested, and then amusement will dissipate the remains of it."

—Samuel Johnson

I am learning that life after a loved one passes is best lived moment to moment for even a day is too long.

There comes a time when the tears stop and you're greeted with the quietness of the agonizing grief waiting to be your companion.

Death is an ending and a beginning. It's how we choose to see it that will help us through the dark nights ahead.

I sometimes wonder where God is in all this death stuff.

I can't understand it, this death and that drives me crazy. Then it dawns on me, it's not about understanding the nature of death but understanding the nature of how I'm living.

I wish I could drown out the sound of the dry earth hitting the top of the casket. It is the sound of finality.

I felt so helpless to help my daughters in their grief. For the first time, I had no answers only my own tears and grief to keep them company.

LET YOUR PAIN AND AGONY BE RECOGNIZED

"The best and most beautiful things in the world cannot be seen nor even touched, but just felt in the heart."
—Helen Keller

I believe I am suffering from a broken heart. Caught off guard, death came in swiftly without a knock on the door to announce its arrival. I wasn't ready. We weren't ready.

Letting go is a shitty feeling. Yet it is the pathway to a new life.

Don't tell me you're sorry. Just hold me and let your heart speak instead of your tongue. I'm sorry just sounds like a broken record after a while.

I wanted to escape the grief but it wouldn't let me go so I stayed and became close friends with it.

There aren't enough tears in my eyes to cry for the loss of losing you.

I called death some pretty horrible names when you died. Now it is a friend I like to sit with for tea to remind me not to live so small.

EXPERIENCE THE FULLNESS OF YOUR TORTURE AND SET IT FREE

"Without you in my arms, I feel emptiness in my soul.
I find myself searching the crowds for your face —
I know it's impossibility, but I cannot help myself."
—Nicholas Sparks

I came face to face with the uncertainty of life and it packs a powerful punch.

My faith at times is challenged during this time of grief.

When will it subside, the agony, the heartbreak, the pain? It seems like it will go on forever.

I don't want to forget your gentle voice, so I saved your voice messages to remind my forgetful mind of what you once sounded like.

There are times that I simply want to claw the pain out of my chest and shake that shit out.

Death have I not seen you enough in two years. Can you please take a break from visiting me?

There's a scream inside that I'm afraid to let go of. It's the holding on that I've been keeping locked up.

It's hard to imagine that grief could uncover so much in such a short time. It's a great detective.

LET COMPASSION WRAP ITS TENDER ARMS AROUND YOUR BRUISED HEART

"No one ever told me that grief felt so like fear."
—C.S. Lewis, A GRIEF OBSERVED

A new uninvited guest has taken up residence in my home. Her name is Grief. She has taken over every square inch of my living quarters without any regard for me. I yell and scream at her to leave and she only stares at me quietly with a strong resistance that says "lady I ain't going nowhere. This here is my home for right now." I let out a barrage of insults in hopes my filthy mouth will do the trick instead she slides over to me and holds me. Big sobs escape my mouth and I just let go and surrender to her ministrations.

I want to dislike God so much right now yet how can I let go of the only true Beloved I have left.

My emotions are like a pendulum. Swinging from sadness, to anger, to grief, and sometimes surprisingly joy sneaks in there.

There is no preparation for what you will feel after a loved one dies. Only being authentic with what arises moment to moment.

I've never felt more vulnerable and powerless than when sitting with a corpse who happens to be the love of your life.

BE KIND TO YOURSELF IN THE DARK MOMENTS OF YOUR SORROW

"You care so much you feel as though you will bleed to death with the pain of it."
—J.K. Rowling, HARRY POTTER AND THE ORDER OF THE PHOENIX

Breathe. Breathe. Hold on. Each breath is a struggle to take in, I am in fear of this new life that has come to me so swiftly. I feel like I am drowning in what I cannot accept.

Oh, how I wish I could take that look of torment out of my daughters' eyes. How I wish I could wipe the memory clean of seeing their father take his last breath so suddenly. There are some things that are beyond the skills of being a mother and better left to God.

God? Are you there?

I want to hold on so tightly to your memory, the attachment of having you, loving you, to what used to be but I know it's in the letting go where I will find life. Yet the heart isn't ready. It isn't ready.

There will be moments in your life where none of your past experiences will prepare you for – death and the loss of a loved one is one of those moments.

In those first few weeks my breath was so painful, so raw, so tortured. I couldn't breathe. Now each breath that I take is a renewal of life.

Death has taught me not to wait for tomorrow. Right now is my whole life. It is my everything.

BELIEVE THAT EACH DAY THE FOG BECOMES THINNER AND THINNER. THERE IS A HEALING TAKING PLACE.

"Give sorrow words; the grief that does not speak knits up the over wrought heart and bids it break."

—William Shakespeare, macbeth

I never experienced true darkness until I received that dreaded phone call. In that instance I came face to face with all my fears that lay hidden under old floorboards.

What is this fear that is gripping me, holding me? It seems to be wrapping itself around me, wanting to be known. What does it want me to know about death? What does it want me to see, to possibly welcome? Perhaps the fear is the fragility of my own humanness. This body isn't forever.

There is so much churning inside of me since the death of my beloved. I am not the same woman. I am not the same woman.

It is so easy to take it for granted, this life. Yet we all want to grab at it with both hands when we are at the end. Please take the time to live your life fully now when you're alive.

I keep finding that parts of me are angry and I acknowledge that anger. Yet I find that my soul simply wants to grow and rejoice. It knows death is the new beginning.

We think death is a fatal sentence. What if it is freedom?

We grieve and mourn not for their passing but for own loss and what that person represented to us. In their death, we begin to see the depths of our attachment.

ONLY DO WHAT INSPIRES YOUR HEART AND SOUL DURING THIS TIME

"Grief is the last act of love we can give to those we loved. Where there is deep grief there was great love."
—Unknown

Sometimes it takes going through all the stages of grief of death and dying to be gifted with a new perspective on life. We find that life is not as vindictive and against us as we thought.

Speak to me of death and I will speak to you of life.

Life is all about growth, opportunity to mature, forgiveness, and our willingness to love ourselves and others unconditionally, even in the darkest moments of our lives. It all belongs.

I see it now with great clarity, grief is a love story unfolding in my aching heart.

I don't know why I've had so much death surround me in the last few years. All I can say is that life is giving me a first-class lesson on letting go and trusting.

Who can be prepared for loss? It's the boomerang in our neat manicure plans we make for ourselves.

GOD HASN'T ABANDONED YOU. SHE IS LIKE THE MOTHER HOLDING AND CRADLING YOUR ANGER, FEARS, AND BROKEN HEART. SEEK HER EVEN WITH YOUR LACK OF UNDERSTANDING.

"I came to realize that my tears were for all the kisses we'll never have again."

I say wait, it will get better. Well, it's been almost a year and it still hurts. When does grief ever end?

There is no returning to normal after the sudden loss of a loved one. Every moment is laced with a new way of being, thinking, speaking, and acting. You are automatically transformed, rewired into a life you never imagined and expected. You are thrown into the lion's den afraid but come out victorious as a warrior.

I've asked myself what does God want from me? Then I ask a different question, does God want anything from me? Sometimes I mistakenly get God confused with being human. Then a puff of clarity comes to me, God isn't in the business of brokering deals, it's only us scared humans that think we can bargain our way out of life challenges.

There are moments in which I can't stand the pain and I want it to leave. But it won't leave, it won't leave and so I surrender to it.

This grief is what is. This pain is what is. These tears are what is. This heartache is what is. In this moment, in this space where everything exists, I am brought fully to a place of awareness.

Slowly, slowly, I thread on this new place where my heart is beating again.

YOU ARE NOT ALONE EVER

"Grief has two parts. The first is loss.
The second is the remaking of life."
—Anne Roiphe

Now I let go of this physical attachment I had for you and open myself to feeling your spiritual nature because you are evermore now.

I keep expecting to see your number when the phone rings. To see your face when the door opens, to hear your laughter when a joke is made. Now I must learn to listen to the stillness and silence to experience your true presence.

I was enjoying a brilliant summer which was cut short by the intrusion of autumn in my life when you suddenly died.

Losing a loved one suddenly breaks open every little crack you already had inside. Now you are wide open to receive. The trick is to recognize the light pouring in during the time of grief.

I wanted to be held in the darkness after you died. To stay in that place of misery where the ripping of my heart seemed to happen every 30 minutes. I wanted to roll around and wallow in the unfairness of life. But there was also a strong part of me pulling me towards another option, the option to live without suffering and to embrace love, openness, cooperation, and yes even joy during this time. It took me a year but I chose life. It felt so much better.

Much of this grief I feel is for what was never finished between us. Now I must journey on my own.

All I wanted to do is bury my head under the covers and sleep, then wake up to the realization that it was all a dream. It's not a dream.

Breathe

"Tears are the silent language of grief."
—Voltaire

Experiencing grief of this magnitude has exposed me to the fragility of my humanity and the strength of my spirit.

People say you're so strong, stay strong, you'll get through this and I think it's the most insensitive thing to say when all I feel is fragile and broken.

The exquisite pain of losing someone so near and dear to you teaches you so much about love. In the beginning, it's the pain that keeps you company then it is the tenderness of love that wraps its arms around you. Permit it all to happen.

Feeling this magnitude of pain and heartache is like a seismic earthquake shaking the roots of my very foundation. Let the cracks happen, let the old descend, allow all that I've held to turn to rubble. When it's all said and done, I'll find myself more resilient and hopeful. God, I hope this isn't BS talk.

During this grief, I've come to realize how much more kindness and love I really need to give to myself. Without it, I am just suffering through each moment. The kindness is like a soft balm being applied to my pain making it feel better. It's like a kiss from grandma saying "honey, it's going to be okay."

One breath, two breaths, three breaths all marching together victoriously.

DENIAL
ANGER
DEPRESSION
BARGAINING
ACCEPTANCE
All are part of the grieving process.

"Sometimes it's okay if the only thing you did today was breathe."
—Yumi Sakugawa

In the beginning, I thought grief was an enemy until it taught me compassion, kindness, love, and grace. It was my reset button.

Each moment sounds off an eternity. It is strange how much can fit into a tiny moment.

I wanted to give up, to stop existing. It felt so natural at times to just say "fuck it, I don't need to be here." This is too hard, bearing the pain of losing a beloved. Then I woke up and realize that it wasn't my destiny to take the easy way out but to stay and honor each pain-filled moment with breath and life. That is my path to healing.

When a loved one dies, we as humans truly come to know our strengths and weaknesses. We come to embrace who we really are, vulnerable fragile beings afraid of death and what's on the other side.

I never understood panic and anxiety attacks until the sudden shock of losing you, they have taken up residence in my body.

Grief is such a selfish bitch. She doesn't care about anyone but herself. She sits and pouts and complains about the pain she's feeling all day long. She goes through dreadful bouts of crying that drowns out all the joy in her waking moments creating rivers and lakes in her path. She cares for nothing but her own sorrow. I hate her.

YES IT FEELS LIKE A HORRIBLE DREAM. HOPING TO WAKE UP TO A DIFFERENT TRUTH.

"The trouble is you think you have time."
—Budhha

I find that each day I am being reborn, learning to creep from this ground on my hands and knees. Finding fresh perspective on things I thought I knew so well. Grief has changed me, each moment I am being invited to open a new door.

Before my grief, I always gave and gave, present for everyone's pain but my own. My boundaries were made out of paper mache. Grief has taught me to only act when inspired, to say no because I can't serve from an empty cup, putting up a sturdier boundary is a must. I must nourish and nurture myself first it said. I must love myself.

It is with great courage that I choose to get up and out of my darkness and visit the light during this time.

They say wait, it will get better, referring to my pain as if it's a storm cloud passing casually over a hot summer's day. If only it was that simple and quick.

Grief has changed me so much. It is a master teacher opening me to the deeper lessons of life that I could not learn before. Each lesson is wisdom I take in.

You were not the only one who died that day. You took a part of me with you and now I don't know who I am.

What if it's not about moving forward after grief but having the courage to live raw, honestly, and authentically? What if it's not about figuring out what the next best step is but having it revealed in its own time? What if you gave yourself to grief and surrendered all those feelings known and unknown? What if you simply let go?

THIS GRIEF THAT YOU FEEL
MAY NEVER LEAVE
BUT IT WILL GIVE YOU
NEW LIFE TO EMBRACE
BEING PRESENT WITH ALL
THE MOMENTS OF YOUR LIFE

"It is difficult to accept death in this society because it is unfamiliar.
In spite of the fact that it happens all the time.
We never see it."

—Elizabeth Kubler-Ross

God, where are you? Where are you? I cannot hear God. I cannot hear God.

Cleaning out our room I came across your shoes and realized that you won't be taking any more steps with me. The shoes were such a reminder that you're no longer here, your footsteps along mine, missed.

Let us go and toss our angriness to the wind. There it will be scattered like seeds in the four directions singing its song "Carry me across the wind and I will take care of your aching heart."

The veil of time has dropped away, now I know that only this moment is real. Only this moment exists. Everything else is an illusion.

I have exploded in a million little pieces, the parts of my old self lost in the wind. Who am I now?

I arrived upon a new shore, this place is desolate, its only inhabitants are sharp rocks that hold memories of yesteryear.

Two funerals happened when you died. Yours and the person I knew as myself.

OPEN YOUR HEART MORE DURING THE PAINFUL DAYS LET IT ACCOMPANY YOU TO THE DEPTHS OF YOUR SORROW

"May love be what you remember most."
—Darcie Sims

Trauma reminds me of walking in the fog and you're scared shit because you can't see anything around you. You are in an abyss without any walls or ground space to hold you in place and keep you safe. Post-traumatic stress is like living in a cloud of fog, a state of limbo that seems to have no beginning and end. All you know is how scared you are that at any moment you're going to die and yet death doesn't surface, only a thousand locust screaming obscenities in your mind wreaking havoc with your sanity. It is a debilitating feeling of fear, panic, and anxiety. I am being tossed like a ship lost at sea, being battered day and night by fierce hurricane gale winds.

May you have the courage to give away your guilt, fears, and unfinished business to God. She is always waiting to accept all parts of you.

I couldn't understand why you left me so suddenly. The only thing I understood was the deep ache in my heart and the silence that took your place.

Each moment I attempted to open that bag you carried, my pain screamed its ugly head through my heart. The agony, the agony is too great. It reminded me that you never made it home.

We pretend that we have so much time to forgive, to laugh, to love, to live fully. Take it from me the only time we have is now. There is no time.

Eventually, there came a time when
I could breathe again and feel the wind
upon my skin and the ground beneath my feet
I began to feel again.

Transformation During Grief

Hope	Light	Grace
Life	Grounded	Faithful
Alive	Accepting	Compassion
Love	Joy	Grateful
Strong	Vulnerable	Free
Filled	Laughter	Beginnings

GOD IS IN YOUR TEARS, PAIN, BROKENNESS, CONFUSION, LONELINESS, AND THE NEXT STEP YOU TAKE

"When you pass through the waters, I will be with you and when you pass through the rivers they will not sweep over you. When you walk through the fire, you will not be burned; the flames will not set you ablaze."

—Isaiah 43:2

I descended into the underworld after months of grief. I was fooled into thinking I was making my way through this grief then more shadows appeared swimming drunkenly around my already tattered self. I cowered in fear, afraid of its ghoulish sounds and this only made them angrier. I found when I could take no more I stood my ground and faced you square on, eye to eye and to my surprise you collapsed at my feet.

I hide the truth so they won't see the wounds that are gaping like black holes in my heart. I am suffering with pain, struggling to find the way back to a place that is no longer there. Where the hell is the new map? I am blind, blind to the next steps, all I have left is simple faith and even that is shaky.

Grief is a degreaser. She cuts all the bullshit that was stuck on your walls, all your self proclaimed knowledge washed down the drain till your walls are left sparkling and brand new with nothing of the old to remind you of that old life.

There is a silence during grief that makes you wonder where God has gone.

I can hardly believe it, I'm a widow now. Oh, how things change at such a fast pace. I never expected to be here so soon, to walk this path in the shadow of the moonlight.

I thought we had so much time but all we ever really had were moments. Oh, how I miss those moments.

DARKNESS SETTLES AND LIGHT COMES TO SHOW IT LOVE

"Forget the former things; do not dwell on the past. See, I am doing a new thing! Now it springs up, do you not perceive it? I am making a way in the desert and streams in the wasteland."

—Isaiah 43 18-19

Shadows, all I see are shadows day and night, night and day. I think I am being followed.

I find that the heart has infinite dimensions that will take a lifetime to explore. It has rooms that have no end, each serving a master that is love.

Don't sweet-talk me into tomorrow, let me have today to grieve, mourn, and lament. Good God please don't rupture another platitude from your mouth, can you not see how they make me feel —unworthy of this moment.

There is no one way to grieve, there is only the grieving. Be honest with it. Be honest with yourself. There is only the truth.

I feel all the depressed sorrowful parts of me coming to the front to be kissed by the light. It has spent so much time in the darkness, naked and afraid to be seen, judged, and laughed at it. It comes forward bearing its teeth and clenching its claws in a defensive manner, fearful of what it finds in the light. It soon realizes that there is nothing to defend or claw at. Grief is just another journey we take in life.

So many create a second funeral for themselves during grief by burying all the pain, emotions, sorrow, disappointments and regrets that come to the surface. Have courage dear heart to let each one have its moment to lament. Don't be so quick to dig another grave.

SURRENDER

"Acceptance is what sets you free to breathe into another moment."

Letting go is so damn hard.

They say to surrender but how do you surrender your heart, the love within it, the memories of yesterday?

It finally dawned on me when I could take no more that all I had left was to let go and let God take over.

Surrendering freed my heart from suffering and freed my mind from anxiety and fear.

Love, it is love that is the cause of so much sadness and pain that I feel and it is worth it. It is worth it.

I realize that I don't have to stop loving you simply because you died. I can love you between the veil and cherish the new space between us.

After a year I can now look at your picture and see your face, your eyes, your lips, and feel your joy skimming through my heart. The wounds are closing.

God, you have ripped my heart out and turned my world upside down. How do I now trust to surrender to this new life you have laid in front of me?

Yes, I say yes to you. For surely you see the bigger picture God where my eyes do not.

Trust is the glue that holds my heart connected to you, Oh Lord.

I realize what I was seeking during my time in grief wasn't to feel better, normal, or to have a mended heart. Rather, it was to recalibrate my trust in the universe, Source, and myself.

I AM FRAGILE VULNERABLE COURAGEOUS

To feel it all.

"Courage is being able to venture into those dark places and bare witness to what greets you there."

I shed my strength for weakness and realized that my weakness was my strength.

I couldn't pretend that I was okay. What a bold-faced lie that would be. People ask me "dear how are you?" and the lazy response is to say "I am okay." But I find I cannot lie anymore, I am not okay. I am in grief.

This vulnerable place I find myself is surprising me. I find it strangely refreshing to be completely authentic with my grief and with people who want to know. I think it makes them uncomfortable.

I've come to realize how very fragile I am. I once thought I was superwoman, now I am just human. Funny how death can reveal the truth so quickly.

From the outside, it looks like I am being broken down but I think I am being rebuilt.

I finally gave myself permission to feel, letting the resistance fall away. It was the best gift I could give to myself.

Today I chose to let go of suffering and choose to grieve honestly from my heart. Suffering is a choice.

AWAKENING ANEW

"I capture the rays of the sun in my face and let the wind caress my skin in a kiss. Yes, life is awakening within me."

I asked myself what did I really want and the only answer that arose within me was joy. I want to taste that sensation again, to be reborn with it. Grief made me forget what it was like to feel it.

I let myself just be still. Giving myself permission to just feel, to just be with all of me, that opened my heart to experience someone I had forgotten about — Me.

Twelve months later I feel. I feel.

Each day is a new beginning after a dance with grief.

This life is finite in the physical sense, show up to it, live, laugh, love, and create the greatest masterpiece of yourself each and every day. Become the greatest version you can daily and give that gift to the world.

I DARE TO LIVE

"What are you doing with life?
That is exactly what death asks you."
—Michael A. Singer, the untethered soul

There is something new tingling from the inside, something I haven't felt in a very long time. Hope.

The grief still lingers in the quiet moments of my heart but the difference one year later is the accepting where I am right now. I've made peace with right now.

I wanted to run so far away from my pain, to ignore its message and pretend that I wasn't aching. But I was aching. Feeling my pain is helping me to reconnect with my heart. I am feeling again.

There's a calming happening. It comes in the guise of laughter. It feels so good to laugh again and let life sprinkle her little joys.

Yes. Yes. Yes. Life is sweet despite the sour notes we might encounter and taste.

I am embracing this new. It is now the path in front of me that I must walk. It is the next chapter.

I've decided to let a few friends accompany me on this next journey of my life, their names are Curiosity, Joy, Love and Playfulness. Death has taught me that life is about living fully.

LIVE

There will be moments in your life where nothing will seem to make sense, where you are left breathless, faithless, confused, heart stricken, numb, lost, and grieving. It is in these moments that you have an opportunity to become the most alive if you allow yourself to feel all of which you are experiencing and honor it honestly. In that moment you will witness your humanity having a truthful conversation with your spirit self and open yourself to the gift of love in the deepest darkest moments of your life.

Thank you
for your bravery

Acknowledgments

There are many over the last three years that have been instrumental in my healing process after Hassel, my husband transitioned. First, and foremost, are my children Jay and Janaya. You both are my inspiration, joy, and great loves. It is through your love that I was truly able to wake up each day and say yes to life. You continue to bring me such joy as our love for each other has grown deeper. I love you!

Second, to my niece Malika who has been my rock during the last three years. I would not have gotten through all those difficult moments without your constant presence to help me pick up the pieces when I could not. Thank you is not enough. I love you dearly.

Third, to the Lake Norman community and the students of Awakenings Yoga Studio. I have never known such a generous community before. You rallied around me and supported me so deeply, compassionately, and authentically. I felt your love and hold it still in my heart. Thank you, thank you for all your love and support.

Fourth, to my siblings Shondella, Mark, Lissette, Ben, and Ronald for holding a sacred container of space for me to heal quietly in my own way. My family in Guyana and Trinidad and Tobago. Aunt Gloria, thank you for coming and caring for me, it meant so much.

Fifth, to my editor Erin Servais, you rock and I am so glad our paths have crossed. Thank you for making these very personal journal entries into a book that may help others see that all parts of the grief process belong. To my publisher Golden Dragonfly Press, thank you for taking this piece on grief and bringing it to life in such a beautiful way. I have learned through you how everything is unfolding in just the right way. Thank you.

Lastly, but certainly not least is the ever-present guidance of a loving God who is guiding, holding, nourishing, and loving me through every dark moment. Even in my anger in not understanding the why, when I wanted to push you away, your presence was ever constant. This whole journey I could not have done without your shepherding. In your mysteries I have come to trust.

ESHA ESTAR

Grief Shaman

Join our community!

We believe that each human life and experience is an opportunity to transcend or move beyond suffering. We believe that how we view things determine our level of suffering.

As a Grief shaman my mission is to guide humanity in reframing our stories/beliefs around grief, death, and loss, a movement towards liberation from suffering.

GO TO WWW.ESHAESTAR.COM TO FIND MANY MORE RESOURCES FOR YOUR JOURNEY INCLUDING:

- Podcast
- Mobile App (coming soon)
- Workbooks on grief, end of life planning, contemplative journals
- Books
- Social media (FB, IG, YouTube)
- Speaking Engagements
- Group Retreats
- One on One with Esha (Mariposa Sanctuary)
- Online courses and teacher trainings

CONNECT ON INSTAGRAM @ESHAESTAR

www.ingramcontent.com/pod-product-compliance
Lightning Source LLC
LaVergne TN
LVHW052257100826
845147LV00001B/73
9781733009959